Usborne Art ideas
Drawing
Animals

INTERNET-LINKED

D0564622

Anna Milbourne

Designed and illustrated by Jan McCafferty,
Doriana Berkovic, Nickey Butler and Non Figg

Managing Editor: Fiona Watt
Managing Designer: Mary Cartwright

Consultant: Gill Figg

Additional illustrations by Catherine-Anne MacKinnon, Gill Figg,
Anna Milbourne, Cristina Adami, Fiona Watt and Christyan Fox
Photographs by Howard Allman; Image manipulation by John Russell
Americanization of text by Carrie Seay

SCHOLASTIC INC.
New York Toronto London Auckland Sydney
Mexico City New Delhi Hong Kong Buenos Aires

Internet links

This book is a self-contained beginner's guide to drawing animals. You do not need a computer to enjoy it, but if you would like to find out more, there are brief descriptions of useful Web sites throughout the book. To visit these Web sites you need to go to the Usborne Quicklinks Web site at **www.usborne-quicklinks.com** Type in the key words 'drawing animals' and you will find direct links to Web sites, as well as pictures and templates for you to download.

What you need

Most of the Web sites listed in this book can be accessed with a standard home computer and an Internet browser (the software that enables you to display information from the Internet). Here's a list of the basic requirements:
– A PC with Microsoft® Windows® 95 or later versions, or a Macintosh PowerPC with System 8.0 or later, and 64Mb RAM
– A browser such as Microsoft® Internet Explorer 4, or Netscape® Navigator 4, or later versions
– Connection to the Internet via a modem (preferably 56Kbps) or a faster digital or cable line
– An account with an Internet Service Provider (ISP)
– A sound card to hear sound files

Extras

Some Web sites need additional programs, called plug-ins, to play sounds, or to show videos, animations or 3-D images. If you go to a site and you do not have the necessary plug-in, a message saying so will come up on the screen. There is usually a button on the site that you can click on to download the plug-in. Alternatively, go to www.usborne-quicklinks.com and click on Net Help. There you can find links to download plug-ins. Here is a list of plug-ins that you might need:
RealPlayer® – lets you play video and hear sound files
Quicktime – enables you to view video clips
Shockwave® – lets you play animations and interactive programs
Flash™ – lets you play animations

Site availability

The links in Usborne Quicklinks are regularly reviewed and updated, but occasionally, you may get a message that a site is unavailable. This might be temporary, so try again later, or even the next day. If any of the recommended sites close down, we will, if possible, replace them with suitable alternatives, so you will always find up-to-date links to sites in Usborne Quicklinks.

Downloadable pictures

Selected pictures, clip art and templates from this book can be downloaded from the Usborne Quicklinks Web site free of charge, for your own personal use.

The pictures must not be copied or distributed for any commercial or profit-related purpose. To find these pictures, go to the Usborne Quicklinks Web site and follow the instructions there.

★ Look out for this star symbol throughout the book. It marks pictures which you can download from the Usborne Quicklinks Web site.

Internet safety

When using the Internet, make sure you follow these guidelines:
– Ask your parent's or guardian's permission before you log on to the Internet.
– If you write a message in a Web site guest book or on a Web site message board, do not include your e-mail address or any other personal information such as your real name, address or telephone number.
– If a Web site asks you to log in or register by typing your name or e-mail address, ask permission of an adult first.
– If you do receive e-mail from someone you don't know, tell an adult and do not reply to the e-mail.
– Never arrange to meet anyone you have talked to on the Internet.

All the sites described in this book have been selected by Usborne editors as suitable, in their opinion, for children, although no guarantees can be given and Usborne Publishing is not responsible for the accuracy or suitability of the information on any Web site other than its own. We recommend that young children are supervised while on the Internet and that children do not use Internet chat rooms.

Computer viruses

A computer virus is a program that can seriously damage your computer. A virus can get into your computer when you download programs from the Internet, or in an attachment (an extra file) that arrives with an e-mail. You can buy anti-virus software at computer stores or download it from the Internet. It is quite expensive, but costs less than repairing a damaged computer. At www.usborne-quicklinks.com you'll find a link to the How Stuff Works Web site where you can find out more about computer viruses.

Getting to the sites

To reach the Web sites described in this book, go to Usborne Quicklinks at **www.usborne-quicklinks.com** and type in the key words 'drawing animals'. Then, follow the instructions given there.

A COMPUTER IS NOT ESSENTIAL
TO USE THIS BOOK
This guide to drawing animals
is a complete, self-contained book.

Contents

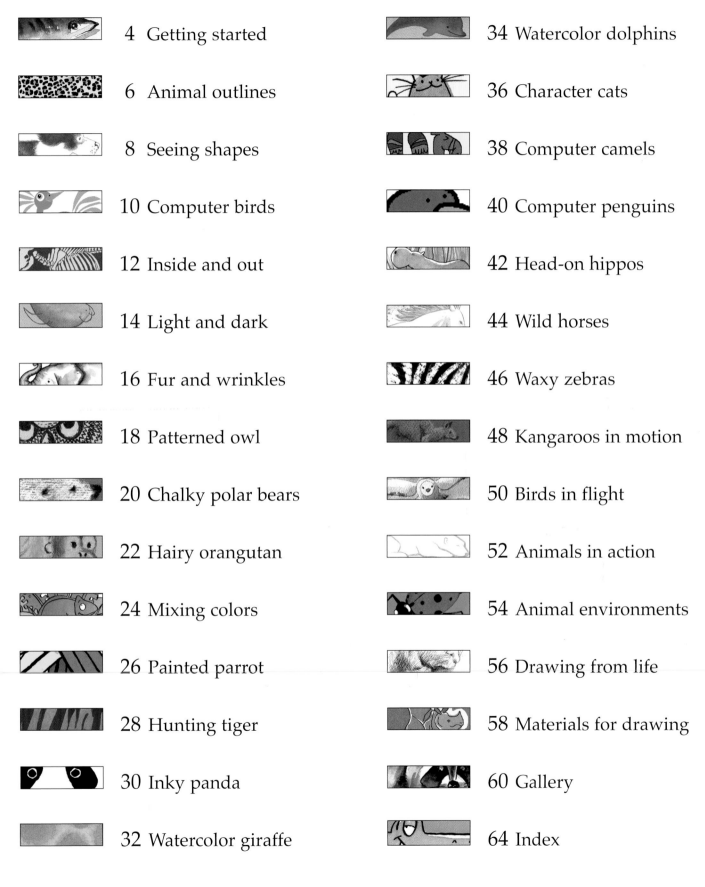

Getting started

All you need to start drawing animals is a pencil and some paper. Look at animals all around you – in real life, wildlife films, photographs, books or on the Web – for inspiration. Here are some ideas of things to do to get started.

Drawing and collecting

Artists keep sketchbooks which they fill with lots of drawings, ideas and information. Keep a folder and fill it with drawings, photographs and pictures of animals to use as reference.

Make quick drawings of animals around you.

Keep unfinished sketches to use as reference.

Collect photographs of wild animals or pets.

4

Materials

Various materials were used to draw and paint the animals in this book. These are explained as you come across them.

Do simple drawings to capture an animal's pose.

Try out materials to get different effects.

Buy postcards of famous paintings from art galleries and shops.

Find out how to draw an orangutan using chalk pastels on pages 22-23.

Find out how to draw cats using a felt-tip pen and watercolor on pages 36-37.

Find out how to paint this panda using a brush and ink on pages 30-31.

🐾 Browse through an online exhibition to see how animals have featured in art through the ages at the **Amarillo Museum of Art** Web site. For a link to this site, go to **www.usborne-quicklinks.com**

Animal outlines

A good way of looking at animals' shapes is by copying their outlines from photos. Try drawing outlines of animals onto black paper to make shadowy shapes. You can get different effects by drawing onto patterned paper.

The silver paper looks like moonlight shining on the fox's tail.

Fox in the moonlight

1. Find a simple picture of an animal to copy. Side views of animals tend to make good, recognizable outlines.

2. Start copying the animal's outline onto black paper. If you make a mistake, don't erase it, just draw a new line.

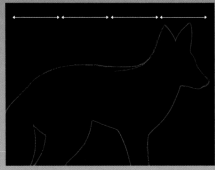

3. As you draw, make sure that the proportions are right. For example, this fox's body is three times as long as its head.

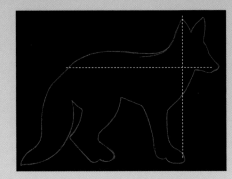

4. At the same time, check which parts of the fox's body line up with each other. This will help get the shape right.

5. When you have finished drawing the outline, cut the shape out. Erase any pencil lines that are left.

6. Lay the fox on some silver foil. Draw around the tip of its tail. Cut this shape out and glue it onto the fox's tail.

Silver paper was added to these animal shapes to make a moonlit scene.

More animal shapes

Try using patterned paper to make animal shapes. You can sometimes find pages in magazines that look like fur or skin, or you could paint paper to look like animal patterns.

★ Throughout this book, stars mark pictures that you can download from the Web to help you draw animals. For example, you can download patterned paper to make these animals. To do this, go to **www.usborne-quicklinks.com**

Giraffes have evenly spaced splotches.

Reptiles have geometrically shaped scales.

Leopards have spots with black outlines.

Seeing shapes

Animals may look complicated to draw because they are all different shapes. You can draw animals more easily if you break them down into simpler shapes, such as circles and triangles. Here are some examples.

There are lots of photographs of different animals at the **Wildlife Gallery** Web site. For a link to this site, go to www.usborne-quicklinks.com

Big cats and domestic cats have similarly shaped bodies.

A rhinoceros' body can be drawn using three overlapping circles.

A penguin's body can be drawn using one oval.

A crocodile's jaws can be drawn using overlapping triangles.

A marmot's body can be drawn using ovals and circles.

An antelope's body can be drawn using overlapping ovals.

Running dog

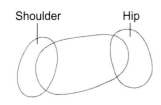

Shoulder Hip

1. In pencil, lightly draw a slanted oval body, with an oval either side for the hip and the shoulder.

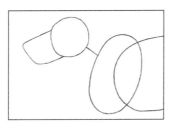

2. Draw the neck as a line coming from the shoulder. Add a circle for the head. Then, add the snout.

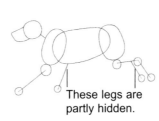

These legs are partly hidden.

3. Draw lines to position the legs. Add small circles for leg joints and paws. Two legs are partly hidden.

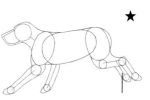

Draw this leg last.

4. Pressing quite lightly, draw an outline around the shapes using smooth, curving lines.

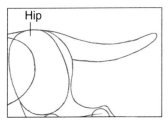

Hip

5. Draw a tail. The tail is a continuation of the backbone, so make it flow from the top of the hip.

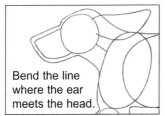

Bend the line where the ear meets the head.

6. Add the ear, starting from the head circle. Then, erase all the shapes inside the outline.

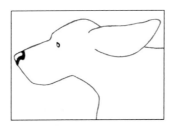

7. Draw the eye. Fill it in, leaving a white circle for a highlight. Fill in the nose, also leaving a highlight.

Add little dots near the nose.

8. Add little lines for fur around the dog's outline. Add patches by filling areas with lots of little lines.

The lines in each patch flow in the same direction.

Some white paper was left showing for a sheen along the dog's back.

A black pencil was used to add the shadow beneath the dog.

9

Computer birds

Computers with Microsoft® Windows® have a program called Paint which you can use for drawing. (Page 58 tells you how to open it.) Paint has shape-drawing tools which can help you draw animals.

Tools and colors

Along the left side of the Paint window, there is a tool box. To draw, you first need to choose a tool. To do this, move your pointer over the tool and click with the left mouse button.

The tool box

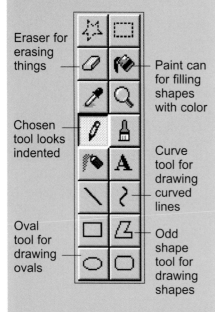

Eraser for erasing things

Chosen tool looks indented

Oval tool for drawing ovals

Paint can for filling shapes with color

Curve tool for drawing curved lines

Odd shape tool for drawing shapes

There is a paint box at the bottom of the Paint window in which you can choose a color to use. To do this, move your pointer over a colored square and click.

The paint box

This box shows the color you have chosen.

Drawing ovals

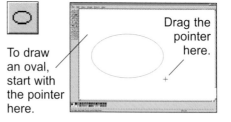

To draw an oval, start with the pointer here.

Drag the pointer here.

Click on the oval tool. Hold the left mouse button down and move the mouse. This is called dragging. Let go of the mouse button to finish the oval.

Curvy lines

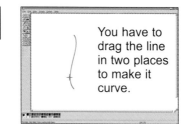

You have to drag the line in two places to make it curve.

Click on the curve tool. Hold the left mouse button down, drag, and let go. Put the pointer on the line and drag it into a curve. Drag it again.

Erasing

You can erase things with the eraser tool. Click on the tool, then hold the left mouse button down and drag the pointer over whatever you want to erase.

Filling in

Make sure the tip of the paint drip is inside the shape.

The shape must have an unbroken outline, or the color will leak out.

To fill a shape with color, click on the paint can tool, and then on a color in the paint box. Move the paint can over the shape and click to fill it in.

Odd shapes

You can draw as many sides as you like.

Click on the odd shape tool. Hold the left mouse button down and drag the mouse to draw a side. Let the button go, then press and drag to make the next side. Double-click to finish the shape.

Draw these shapes big.

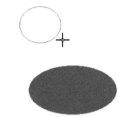

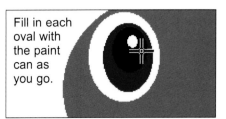 Fill in each oval with the paint can as you go.

1. Click on blue, then on the oval tool. Draw an oval body and a smaller oval head above it. Fill them in with blue.

2. Use the curve tool to draw two curved lines for the neck, connecting the body to the head. Fill the neck in with blue.

3. For the eye, draw a white oval. Add a blue one inside it and a black one inside that. Do a tiny white oval for a highlight.

Make sure there are no gaps before filling the feathers.

Add a wing shape using the curve tool.

4. Click on orange. Use the odd shape tool to draw a beak and two legs. Use the paint can to fill them in.

5. Use the curve tool to draw one side of a feather. Draw another curve for the other side. Fill them with orange.

Add a nostril using the oval tool.

Try drawing different birds with these tools. Find out how to draw more animals with Paint on pages 38-41.

Making mistakes

If you make a mistake, then you can undo it. Hold the CTRL key down and press Z. To get rid of everything on your page, hold the CTRL key down, press N, then click on *No* in the box that appears.

11

Inside and out

It helps to understand a little about what animals' insides look like, to be able to draw their outsides. Although animals all look so different, there are similarities in the way their bodies work. There are also a couple of tricks that can help you work out their shapes.

Animals and people

There are similarities between a four-legged animal's skeleton and a person's skeleton. Comparing the two can help you work out which way animals bend their legs.

On this drawing of a cow (from 'Three cows') by Pisanello, you can see where its bones stick out, especially along the spine.

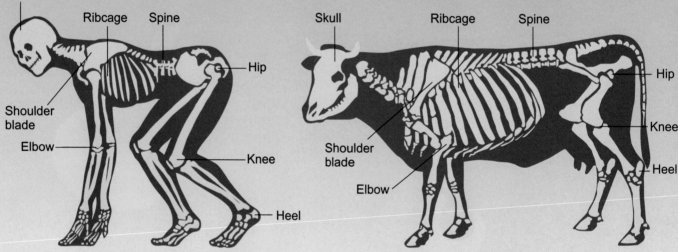

This man is on all fours, so that you can see the similarities between his skeleton and the cow's.

The cow skeleton has the same labels as the man, so that you can compare their joints.

Zigzag legs

A handy trick for drawing animals' legs is to imagine a zigzag shape inside them. Most four-legged animals have a zigzag leg shape. There's more about zigzag legs on page 48.

The zigzags show where the bones are.

The zigzags are different shapes in different poses.

Bony cow

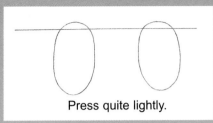

Press quite lightly.

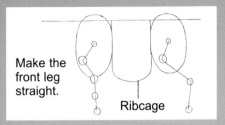

Make the front leg straight.

Ribcage

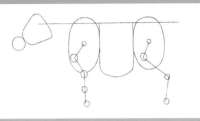

1. In pencil, draw a straight line for the spine, with a big oval near each end for the shoulder and hip bones.

2. Add a curved line between the ovals for the ribcage. Add zigzag legs with circle joints from the shoulder and the hip.

3. For the head, do a rounded triangle, and a circle. The spine is a little higher than the middle of the triangle.

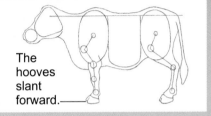

The hooves slant forward.

★

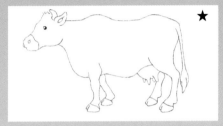

★

4. Draw an outline around the shapes, like the one above. Draw the tail, making it flow from the cow's back.

5. You can only see part of the cow's other legs. Draw leg lines with circle joints on them first, then draw their outlines.

6. Erase the extra lines. Add an udder. Draw an ear, horns and a nostril. Add an eye. Fill it in, leaving a white dot inside it.

The background was filled in using colored pencils.

Patches were added to this cow using black colored pencil.

🐾 Look at some marvellous photos and paintings of cows at to the **Allcows** Web site. For a link to the site, go to **www.usborne-quicklinks.com**

White parts were left on the hooves to show highlights.

Light and dark

Adding areas of light and dark, or shading, can help make your drawing look solid and three-dimensional. This section shows two different ways of shading, using pencil and ink.

The light is coming from here.

Light and shape

When light shines on something, the parts facing the light are palest; the parts facing away from the light are darkest. By adding light, medium and dark areas, you can make a drawing look solid.

★

Darkest area

Medium area

Lightest area

The snails' shadows fall away from the light.

Smooth blend seal

Erase the lines that overlap the flippers and tail.

Add some lines to the flippers.

Add dark shading under the body and on the back and tail.

1. Draw a seal shape as shown above. Start with the big teardrop body and then add the flippers, tail and face.

2. Shade the body by pressing lightly with a pencil and filling the shape in. Leave the lightest areas white.

3. Go over the areas you want to be dark, pressing harder. Press lighter as you reach the medium areas to blend the two.

Ink wash fish

The two shades will blend together on the damp paper.

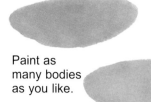

Paint as many bodies as you like.

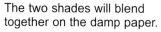

1. In a saucer, mix blue ink with lots of water to make a pale shade. Then, paint the oval bodies of the fish.

2. Add more ink to the saucer, and, while the fish bodies are still damp, paint the darker shade on their undersides.

3. When the fish are totally dry, use a blue fountain pen or felt-tip pen to draw their outlines, faces and scales.

14

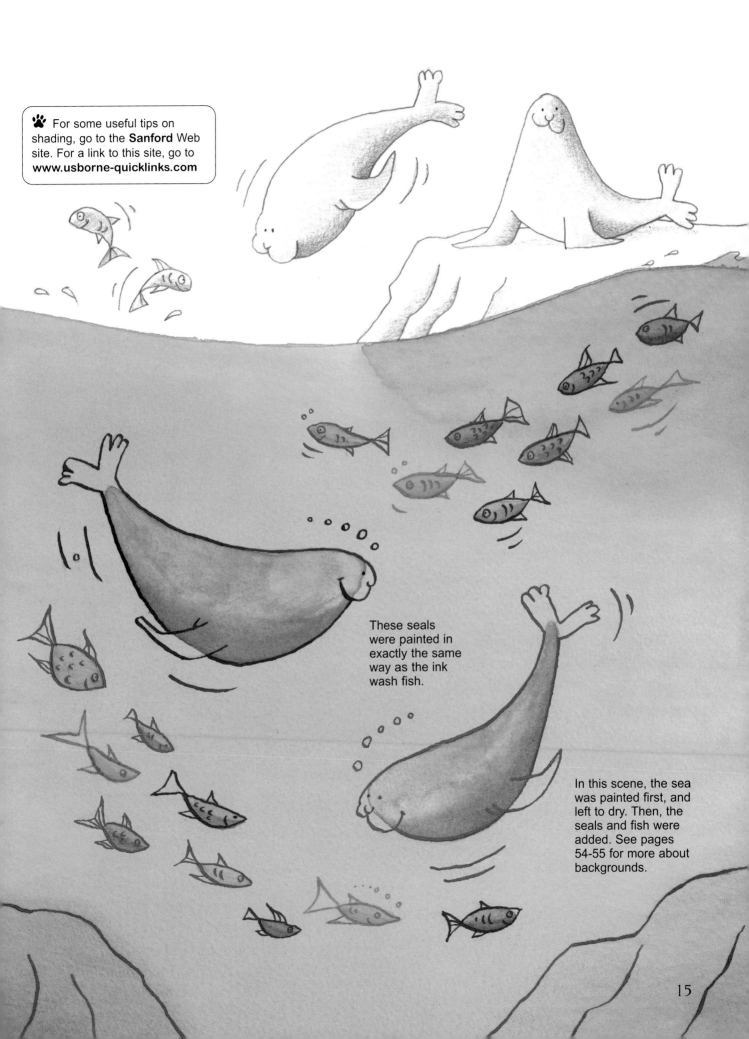

For some useful tips on shading, go to the **Sanford** Web site. For a link to this site, go to **www.usborne-quicklinks.com**

These seals were painted in exactly the same way as the ink wash fish.

In this scene, the sea was painted first, and left to dry. Then, the seals and fish were added. See pages 54-55 for more about backgrounds.

15

Fur and wrinkles

Animals have all sorts of different textures, from shaggy fur to wrinkly skin. As you are shading an animal, there are various ways in which to draw its fur, feathers, skin or scales.

Use long, straight lines for bristly fur.

Use wavy lines and patterns for a shell and reptile skin.

Use curly lines for wool.

In his painting, 'A Young Hare', Albrecht Dürer uses lots of paintbrush strokes to show the texture of the animal's fur.

Furry mouse

The teardrop should tilt upward.

1. Pressing very lightly with a pencil, draw a teardrop shape for the mouse's body. Then, add ears, an eye and the tail.

Adding less texture in the light parts and more in the dark parts shows the animal's shape.

A shadow was added under the mouse.

Erase this extra line.

2. Add a curve inside the teardrop shape for the head. Draw a curve for the back leg and draw two little feet.

16

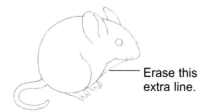

The lines show which way the fur lies.

3. Do lots of tiny lines on the body. Do more lines to make darker areas. Leave the lightest areas white.

4. Using a dark pencil, do lines in the darkest areas. Add lines on the tail. Color the mouse's eye black, but leave a highlight.

Wrinkly elephant

1. Using pencil, draw an oval body and a smaller oval head. Draw zigzag leg lines with circles for joints. Add oval feet.

The trunk curls back and touches the head.

2. Add a triangular ear. Draw two lines for the trunk curling up into the air. Add a line for the tail.

When the paper is dry, you may have to re-draw parts of the outline if the water has washed it away.

The watery ink shows the elephant's shape and the pen lines show its wrinkles.

🐾 Browse through a gallery of lovely elephant photos at the **Project Elephant** Web site. For a link to this site, go to **www.usborne-quicklinks.com**

★

3. Draw the outline in water-soluble felt-tip pen. Add an eye. Then, erase the pencil lines.

4. Wet a paintbrush and paint water under the elephant's belly, touching the outline. The ink will spread.

5. Paint touches of water elsewhere on the elephant, spreading the color to shade the body.

6. Let the drawing dry. Then draw lines to show wrinkles. Do curves around the knees and trunk.

Patterned owl

One good way of drawing animal textures is to simplify them into patterns. This can have a dramatic effect. Varying the thickness of the line you use can add to the effect. Use a thin and a thick felt-tip pen to draw this owl.

This shows how you can draw different patterns to show feathers either realistically or in a simplified style.

Short lines or zigzags show feathers around the eyes.

Breast feathers are shorter and rounder like this.

Rows of dashes show head feathers.

Wing feathers are leaf shapes with lines inside them.

This painting 'Roosters' by Ito Jakuchu shows how simple patterns can be used to show lots of different types of feathers.

The body is twice as long as the head.

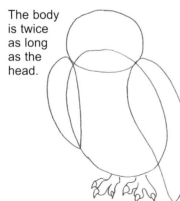

1. Draw a slanted oval for the owl's body, and another oval for its head. Add wing shapes. Then add clawed talons.

Leave ragged edges on the tissue shapes.

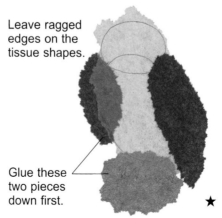

Glue these two pieces down first.

★

2. Using tissue paper, tear out a shape for the head and body, two wings and a tree stump. Glue them onto the drawing.

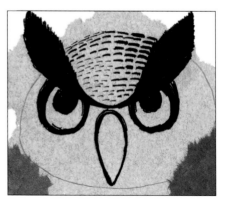

3. With a black felt-tip pen, draw the beak, tufts and eyes. Fill them in. Do lines across the head in thin and thick felt-tip.

18

 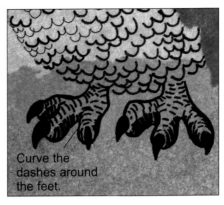 

4. Using a thin and a thick felt-tip pen, do zigzag lines around the eyes. Add slanted lines and nostrils on the beak.

5. Draw downy breast feathers with curved lines in thin and thick felt-tip pen. Outline the feet and draw dashes on them.

6. Use a thick felt-tip pen to fill the wing shapes with long feathers. Add lines to them and fill in the tips.

Curve the dashes around the feet.

Start at the top of the wings and work down.

Patterns curving around the head and breast show the owl's shape.

This moon was torn out of tissue paper.

Different patterns on different areas of the owl show the various textures of its feathers.

🐾 Use colored felt-tip pens to draw a patterned bird in a cherry tree at the **Sanford** Web site. For a link to this site, go to **www.usborne-quicklinks.com**

Chalky polar bears

You can draw these polar bears using chalk pastels to get a soft, furry effect. The bears' white fur and their snowy surroundings means you only need black and white chalk pastels to create the picture. Chalk pastels are crumbly and smudgy, but easy to use.

 See some beautiful photographs of polar bears at the **Polar Bears Alive** Web site. For a link to this site, go to **www.usborne-quicklinks.com**

Chalk pastels work well on colored paper.

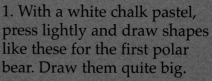

Leave room for another bear on the right.

1. With a white chalk pastel, press lightly and draw shapes like these for the first polar bear. Draw them quite big.

The neck slopes down here.

Take care around the overlapping nose.

2. To the right of the first bear, draw the shapes for the second one. Make its nose overlap the first bear.

3. Draw the bears' outlines around the shapes with smooth, curved lines. Add arches for their legs.

4. Use a small piece of black chalk pastel on its side to fill in some dark areas on the two polar bears, like this.

Rest your hand on a scrap of paper to avoid smudging your picture as you draw.

5. Use a white chalk pastel on its side to color the light areas. Go right up to the black parts with the white color.

6. Using your finger, gently smudge the black and white together. The smudged part will turn gray.

7. To show the bears' fur, do short, slanted lines in black all over the gray areas, and also around the black edges.

Go around the ears in white.

8. In white, do more slanted lines in the gray areas and also around the white edges, to show the fluffy white fur.

9. Do a little black mark for each eye and semicircles for the ears. Color the tips of the noses in black.

10. Draw some hills in black and white. Add shadows under the bears' feet. Blend them gently with your finger.

Blue paper helps the scene look icy and cold.

You will need to 'fix' your drawing so that it won't smudge. See page 59 for how to do this.

The bears' shadows are like blurry reflections.

Hairy orangutan

Chalk pastels can be used to show different kinds of texture. For example, you can blend two or three colors together to show an orangutan's skin, and you can use unblended lines to show the long hair on its body.

Draw in the middle of the paper. Press lightly to make pale lines.

The circles line up diagonally.

1. With an orange chalk pastel, draw three circles on green paper, as shown here.

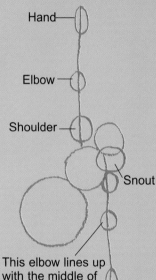

Hand

Elbow

Shoulder

Snout

This elbow lines up with the middle of the biggest circle.

2. Add a circle for the snout. Draw lines for arms, then add circular joints and oval hands.

3. Draw two bent lines for legs. Then, add circular knees and oval feet.

★

Add a branch in brown pastel.

These fingers curl around the branch.

4. Draw the outline, like this, going around the arms and legs. Add fingers and toes.

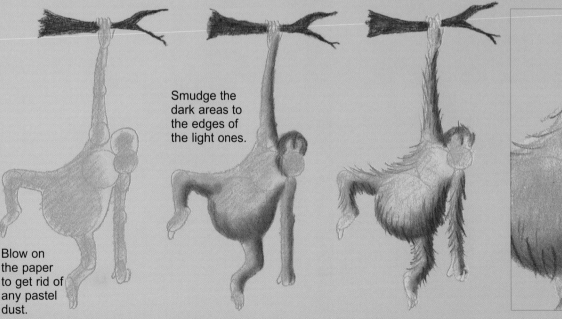

Blow on the paper to get rid of any pastel dust.

5. With a pale orange pastel, fill in these areas. Blend them in with your finger.

Smudge the dark areas to the edges of the light ones.

6. Fill in the dark areas with a brown pastel. Blend them in with your finger.

7. Add hair with orange and brown pastels. Use long lines and don't blend them.

8. Add a little pink on the face, chest and belly and blend it in with your finger.

22

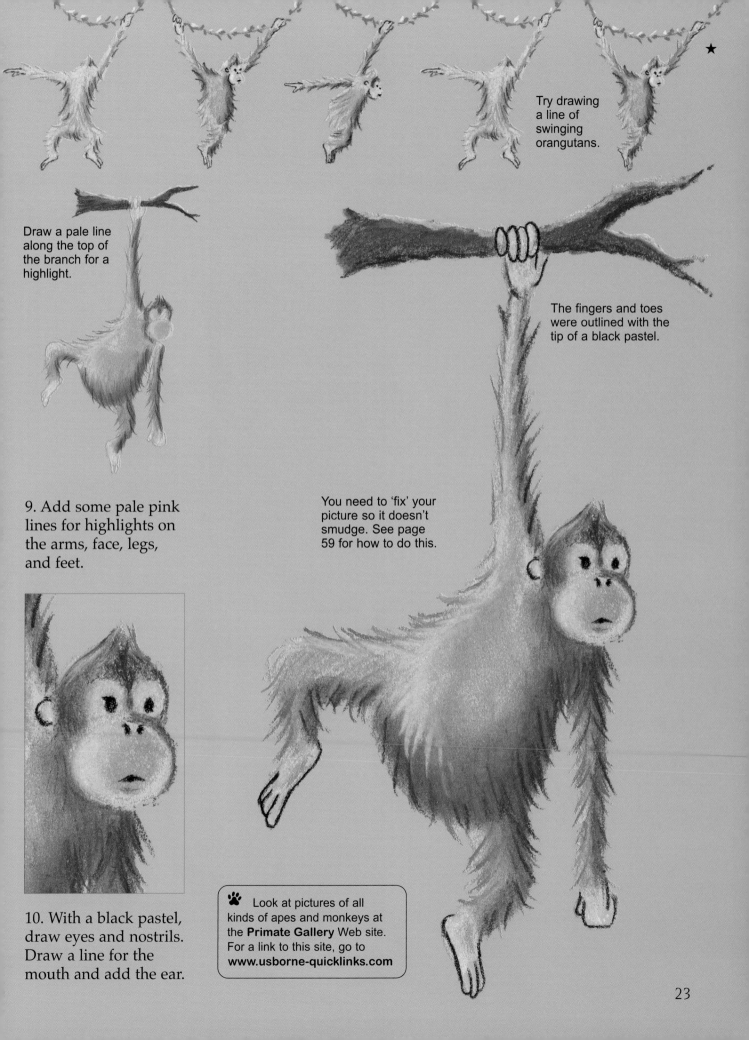

Try drawing a line of swinging orangutans.

Draw a pale line along the top of the branch for a highlight.

The fingers and toes were outlined with the tip of a black pastel.

9. Add some pale pink lines for highlights on the arms, face, legs, and feet.

You need to 'fix' your picture so it doesn't smudge. See page 59 for how to do this.

10. With a black pastel, draw eyes and nostrils. Draw a line for the mouth and add the ear.

Look at pictures of all kinds of apes and monkeys at the **Primate Gallery** Web site. For a link to this site, go to **www.usborne-quicklinks.com**

23

Mixing colors

The animal world is full of color, from bright parrots to patterned tabby cats. Knowing how to mix different colors will help you make the most of animals' colors in your drawings.

🐾 Play an art detective game to explore the use of color in paintings at the **Sanford** Web site. For a link to this site, go to **www.usborne-quicklinks.com**

Bare necessities

There are three basic colors which you cannot make by mixing other colors: red, yellow and blue. These are called primary colors. Using these three colors, you can mix almost any other color you will need.

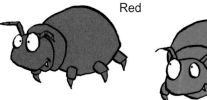 Red   Blue

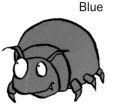 Yellow

All mixed up

By mixing primary colors together you can make more colors: orange, green and purple. These are secondary colors. By altering how much of each color you use in the mix, you can make different shades of these colors.

The beak on the toucan above was painted mixing red and yellow together to make shades of orange.

The circle is a color wheel. It shows how colors are related to one another.

★

Yellow and red at either end of this snake mix to make shades of orange.

Blue and yellow at either end of this snake mix to make shades of green.

Red and blue at either end of this snake mix to make shades of purple.

This snake was painted using all the colors on the color wheel.

Blending in

Some animals have colors which blend in with their surroundings. Use colors next to each other on the color wheel to show this.

Showing off

Some animals have colors which stand out against their surroundings. Use colors from opposite sides of the color wheel, such as red and green, to show this. These colors look brighter when next to each other.

A chameleon can change color to match the leaves. This helps it hide.

This red poison arrow frog stands out against the green leaves.

Mixing shades

If you mix all three primary colors together, they make neutral colors like brown. Start with a mixture of two primary colors and add the third bit by bit to mix these shades.

Mix red and yellow.

Add a dab of blue.

Add more blue.

Add more blue.

Mix blue and yellow.

Add a dab of red.

Add more red.

Add more red.

Mix blue and red.

Add a dab of yellow.

Add more yellow.

Add more yellow.

Lighter and darker

If you add white to colors you can make them lighter. You can make colors darker by adding black, but this also makes them duller. Sometimes adding another color, such as blue, can work better.

This armadillo was painted brown.

White was added to the brown to make this color.

Blue was added to the brown to make this color.

25

Painted parrot

To paint this parrot you only need paints in the primary colors: red, yellow and blue. All the other colors can be mixed from these. This picture can be painted with poster paints or acrylics.

🐾 Look at photos of lots of different types of colorful parrots on the **PhotoArt of Nature** Web site. For links to this site, go to **www.usborne-quicklinks.com**

Acrylics and poster paints

Poster paints and acrylics are both good for painting solid areas of color. Here are some tips on how to use them.

Use your brush to dab some of the paint onto a saucer. Mix water into the paint to make it runnier and easier to paint with.

Rinse your brush well before using another color.

Don't let the paint dry on your brush, or it will ruin the bristles.

To mix a new color, first put dabs of the colors you are mixing onto a plate. Mix the paints together in the middle of the plate, little by little, until you get the color you want.

Once acrylic or poster paint is dry, you can paint on top of it with another color.

The wings cross over each other.

★

1. Using a pencil, draw a big oval for the body, and a circle for the head. Then, add the wing and tail feathers.

2. Connect the shapes like this. Draw big, jagged feathers. Add a beak, an eye and a perch.

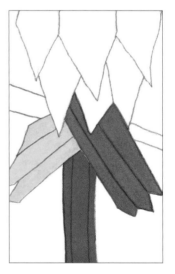

3. Mix a drop of water into some red paint and paint the parrot's head and tail feathers. Let them dry.

4. Rinse your brush and paint the yellow feathers. Let them dry. Rinse your brush and paint the blue feathers.

The black outline is thicker in some places than others.

5. Mix a little yellow with the same amount of red to make orange. Paint the orange feathers.

More colors were mixed to paint these flowers and leaves.

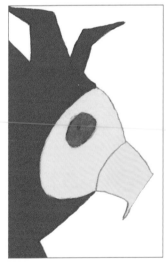

6. Rinse your brush. Mix a little blue and the same amount of yellow to make green. Paint the last feathers.

7. Mix a small amount of yellow, blue and red together to make brown. Paint the parrot's perch.

8. Mix yellow with water to make it pale. Paint the beak and face. When it's dry, paint a brown eye.

9. Leave the painting to dry. Then, go around the outlines of your parrot with a black felt-tip pen.

27

Hunting tiger

Many animals have patterned coats, so that they can either hide or hunt without being seen. The background of a drawing can emphasize this. Using different shades of the same colors for the animal and its surroundings helps the animal blend in. See page 25 for tips on mixing different shades.

In his painting 'Tiger in a Tropical Storm (Surprised!)', Henri Rousseau uses shapes and colors to help the tiger blend in.

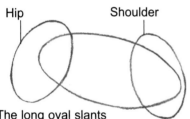

Hip   Shoulder

The long oval slants down to the right.

1. Draw a long oval for the tiger's body. Add another two ovals overlapping it for the hip and shoulder.

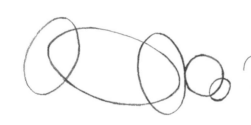

2. Add a circle for the head. It should be halfway down the shoulder oval. Add a small oval muzzle.

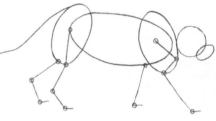

3. Draw zigzag lines for the legs with circles for joints. Draw a line for the tail from the top of the hip oval.

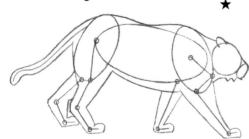

Add an ear far back on the tiger's head.

★

Look at the main picture to see where to put the white parts.

4. Draw the tiger's outline. Erase the extra lines inside the outline, and then draw lines to show the white parts.

28

5. Draw a grass shape behind the tiger. Add blades of long grass overlapping the tiger and leaves in the foreground.

You can let the green paint overlap the grass stems slightly.

6. Mix some green paint and paint the background. Use watery green to paint the area below the tiger. Let it dry.

7. Mix orange using red and yellow paint. Paint the tiger. Paint its belly and the flashes on its head white.

8. When the tiger is dry, paint its stripes in dark brown. Paint the tiger's eye, nose and mouth in black.

9. Mix a range of different greens and browns (see page 25). Paint simple grass and leaf shapes in different shades.

This tiger was painted using acrylic paints.

Details on the leaves and grass were added in brown and green.

Inky panda

You can use a brush and ink to do simple paintings of animals. Using watery and strong shades of two colors can give a striking effect. Use a soft brush with a pointed tip for this type of picture.

Using inks

Colored inks come in bottles or cartridges. You can cut off the end of a cartridge and squeeze the ink onto a saucer.

Use ink straight from the bottle or cartridge for a strong shade.

Dab lots of water onto a saucer, then dab a little ink into it to mix a pale shade.

Ink is very runny. Dip your brush in the ink, then dab it on a paper towel before painting, so it doesn't drip.

Rinse your brush well and dry it before using a different color.

1. Mix watery black ink. Paint the panda's head and body, using a smooth, flowing line. Leave it to dry.

3. Use undiluted black ink on the very tip of your brush to paint little, round eyes and a nose. Leave them to dry.

Make the paws shaggy around the edges.

2. Use undiluted black ink to paint the ears. Paint a stripe over the chest, then add the arms and legs. Let them dry.

The patches slope outward at the bottom.

4. Paint the panda's eye patches in undiluted black ink. Leave a little white circle around each eye.

Bamboo

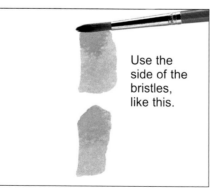

Use the side of the bristles, like this.

1. Mix watery green ink and paint a section of bamboo stem. Paint sections above it, leaving gaps between them.

Let the stems dry before adding the leaves in undiluted ink.

2. Use one brush stroke for each leaf. Press lightly with the tip of the brush, then press harder, and then lightly again.

🐾 Go to the **Panda Central** Web site to see photographs and videos of a baby panda growing up. For a link to this site, go to **www.usborne-quicklinks.com**

The joints on the stems were painted in undiluted ink when the stems were dry.

The grass was painted in the same way as the leaves.

Watercolor giraffe

Painting tips

Watercolor paints come in either tubes, or blocks called pans. Here are some tips on using them.

With pans, rub a wet brush on the pan to get paint on the bristles. Dab the paint onto a saucer.

With tubes, squeeze a tiny blob from the tube onto a saucer, and add water with your brush.

Add more water to make the color paler.

Wet watercolors blur together.

Let a color dry before adding the next one if you don't want them to blur.

Watercolor paints are good for adding color to drawings without hiding the original outline. If you want to draw the outline of an animal before painting it, you need to use a permanent pen – one which doesn't run when it gets wet.

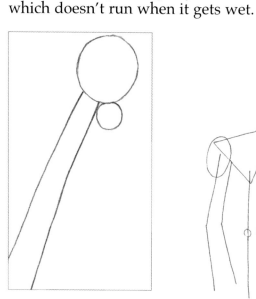

1. Start near the top of the paper. In pencil, draw two circles for the head and muzzle and two long lines for the neck.

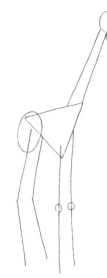

2. Draw a triangular body with an oval hip. Add four long stick legs. Put circles halfway down the front legs.

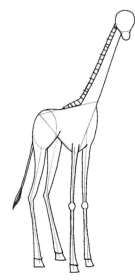

3. Draw the giraffe's outline in permanent pen. Make the knees knobby. Add the hooves, a mane and a tail.

4. Add ears, horns, eyes with semicircular eyelids, and curly nostrils. Then, erase the pencil lines.

Don't worry about it being neat.

5. Draw a low hill and a tree. Mix yellow watercolor with a little red and fill in the giraffe's shape.

The orange splotches will blur on the damp paper.

6. Mix a bright orange. Dab splotches all over the giraffe's body while the paper is still damp.

7. Paint the mane and tail orange, and the hooves and horns grey. Dampen the background a little and paint it. Let the colors blur together.

When the paint is dry, you could add a pen line around the picture to frame it.

See pages 54-55 for tips on painting backgrounds.

★

Look at a blurry watercolor painting of a cat at the **Fountain Studio** Web site. For a link to this site, go to **www.usborne-quicklinks.com**

You can do all kinds of animals using this technique. Draw quickly. If the lines are a little lopsided it gives the animal more character.

The blurry effect can add to the picture. Here, the pink from the flamingo has spread into the water and looks like a reflection.

★

Paint a very simple background to make the animal stand out.

Watercolor dolphins

When painting with watercolors, you can build up color gradually in layers, or washes. You can get different effects by painting onto wet or dry paper. It's best to use watercolor paper (see page 59) for this dolphin picture, but if you don't have any, you can use thick Bristol paper instead.

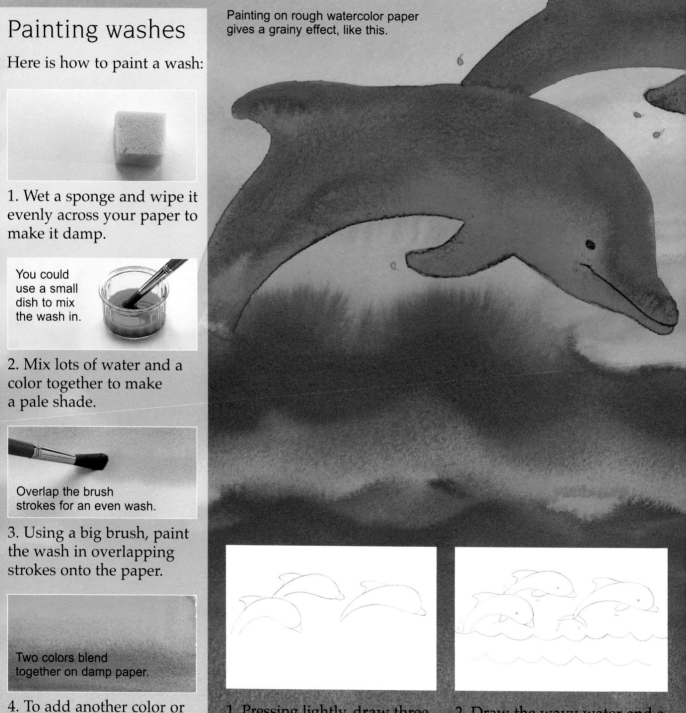

Painting washes

Here is how to paint a wash:

1. Wet a sponge and wipe it evenly across your paper to make it damp.

You could use a small dish to mix the wash in.

2. Mix lots of water and a color together to make a pale shade.

Overlap the brush strokes for an even wash.

3. Using a big brush, paint the wash in overlapping strokes onto the paper.

Two colors blend together on damp paper.

4. To add another color or shade to the wash, paint it onto the damp paper.

Painting on rough watercolor paper gives a grainy effect, like this.

1. Pressing lightly, draw three curved teardrop shapes with a blue pencil. Then, add the dolphins' beaks and fins.

2. Draw the wavy water and a few droplets. Draw one dolphin's tail. The other tails are hidden. Add their flippers and eyes.

Look at photographs of dolphins and whales at **David's Whale and Dolphin Watch** Web site. For a link to this site, go to **www.usborne-quicklinks.com**

Paint the water droplets in blue, like the sea.

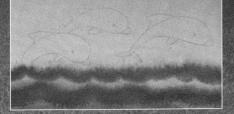

Waves painted on damp paper have soft, blurry edges.

A shape painted on dry paper has clear, sharp edges.

The blue will blend in with the green on the damp bodies.

3. Paint a pale green wash over the paper. Then, add blue waves to the sea while the paper is damp. Let it dry.

4. Mix blue, a little yellow and lots of water to make a blue-green wash. Fill in each dolphin with the wash.

5. Mix blue paint with water, and paint the tops of the damp bodies. Let them dry. Add the eyes and mouths in black pencil.

35

Character cats

Cartoonists and illustrators have drawn animals in various ways, often giving them amusing characters. The scene below was created by drawing lots of cats, all with different expressions.

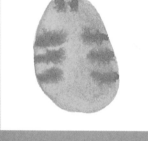

1. Using watercolor paints, mix a watery orange color. Paint an oval body. It needn't be too neat.

2. Mix a brighter shade of orange for some stripes. Paint them while the paper is still a little damp.

3. When the cat is dry, draw an outline in fine felt-tip pen. Add lines for the front legs and oval paws with claws.

4. Draw a face, some whiskers and a tail. Draw quickly – it adds character if it's a little lopsided.

Expressions

By changing the size, shape and the faces on the cats you can give them different characters. Here are a few ideas.

A fat cat has a small, high face.

A scared cat has circles with dots in them for eyes.

Caterwauling cats have closed eyes high on their heads and open mouths.

A cross cat has slanted lines above its eyes.

Edward Lear, an artist and an author of nonsense poetry, drew his cat, Foss, in all sorts of comical poses. Here are three examples.

Foſs, a untin.

Foſs dansant

Foſs rampant

🐾 Browse through an online exhibition to see how cats have featured in art throughout the ages at the **Cats In Art** Web site. For a link to this site, go to **www.usborne-quicklinks.com**

The watercolor background was painted before the cats for this scene. See page 55 for how to do backgrounds.

Gray shapes were painted for trashcans, and then the outlines and details were added in pen.

Computer camels

The computer program Paint has tools which enable you to draw an animal and then copy it again and again. (To open Paint, see page 58). You can find out how to use the brush tool below, but look at page 10 for how to use the other tools you'll need to draw these camels.

Drawing an outline

To draw, click on the brush tool. Click on a brush style in the options (see below) to choose a type of line to use. Position the pointer over the white screen, hold the left mouse button down and drag the mouse.

Brush tool

When you click on the brush tool, these options appear below the tool box.

The camels were drawn using this brush style.

Camel train

Don't draw the head too big.

Make sure the outline has no gaps in.

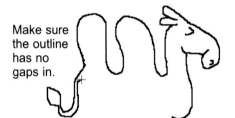

1. Click on a small brush style. Draw the camel's ears and nose. Add the jaw. Then, draw two curves for the neck.

2. Add an eye and nostril. Draw two humps. Draw the top side of the tail upto the tip. Then, add the rest of the tail.

3. Draw the front leg – first draw the part from the neck to the middle of the toes, then the rest. Add the belly.

Start the rectangle here.

A dotted line will appear.

Finish the rectangle here.

4. Draw the back leg. Then, add the other two legs under the belly. Make sure there are no gaps in the outline.

5. Draw reins and patterns on the humps. Click on the eraser tool. Erase the line where the reins overlap the body.

You'll need to erase this line.

6. Click on the select tool. Put your pointer above and left of the camel. Hold the left mouse button and drag out a rectangle.

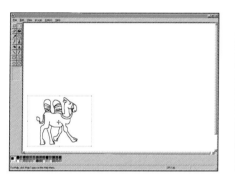

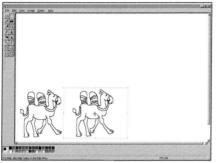

7. Position your pointer over the camel. Holding the left mouse button down, drag the camel to the left of the screen. Let go of the mouse button.

8. Holding down the CTRL key on the keyboard, drag the camel to the right. It will leave a copy. Let go of the CTRL key and the mouse button.

9. Make more copies of the camel. Then, click on the paint can tool. Click on different colors and parts of the camels to color them in.

Here, a background of sand dunes was drawn in behind the camel train.

You might only be able to fit three camels across your screen – it depends on the size of your screen.

Remember if you make mistakes you can undo them. See pages 10-11 for how.

39

Computer penguins

Using the computer program Paint, you can draw a group of animals by copying one animal again and again, and flipping some of the copies over to face the other way. See page 58 for how to open Paint, and pages 10 and 38 for how to use some of the tools you'll need.

A colony of penguins

Click on this brush style.

1. Click on the black color. Click on the brush tool. Below the tool box, click on the medium round brush style.

2. To draw, press the left mouse button and drag the mouse. Draw a head, a beak, a wing, a tail and a body.

3. Draw the other wing. Draw feet under the body. Add a line on the body. Click to make a dot for each eye.

Make sure there are no gaps in the outline.

4. Click on blue, then click on the paint can tool. Click on the penguin to color it blue. Color the belly pale yellow.

5. Click on orange in the paint box, and then click on the penguin's beak and feet to color them orange.

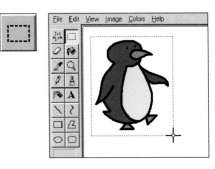

6. Click on the select tool. Pressing the left mouse button down, drag a box around the penguin.

You could draw some smaller penguins in the scene, too.

Click on this option.

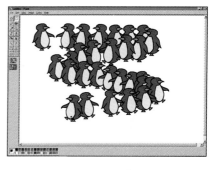

7. Click on the bottom option below the tool box. Pressing the CTRL key on the keyboard, drag the penguin to make a copy. Let the mouse button go.

8. Click on *Image* at the top of the screen. On the list that appears click on *Flip/Rotate*. In the box, click on *Flip horizontal*, and then on *OK*.

9. Copy and flip the penguin a few more times to make a whole colony. Use the brush and paint can tools to add icy hills in the background.

Head-on hippos

Animals look completely different shapes from the front than from the side. From the front, parts of an animal may be hidden by the rest of its body. Its body looks shorter than it actually is. This is called foreshortening.

See how hippos have featured in art through the ages, and look at pictures of famous hippos at the **Hippo World** Web site. For links to this site, go to **www.usborne-quicklinks.com**

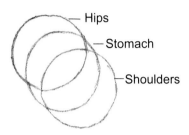

Hips

Stomach

Shoulders

1. In pencil, draw three overlapping circles for the hips, stomach, and shoulders.

2. Draw two circles in front for the head and nose. Add the eyes, nostrils and ears.

3. Draw front legs from the shoulder and a back leg from the hip.

4. Draw the outline, using the circles to show the fat body. Erase the extra lines.

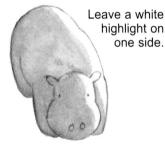

Leave a white highlight on one side.

Dab the pink on while the paint is damp.

5. Paint the hippo with brown watercolor, making one side darker than the other.

6. Add a little pink to the mouth and eyes. Let it dry. Draw the outline with a fine felt-tip pen.

The grass was painted with green watercolor. When it was dry, the black lines were added using a felt-tip.

The background was painted around the hippos before the outlines were added. See page 55 for how to do this.

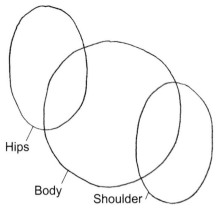

Hips

Body Shoulder

1. In pencil, draw an oval for the hips, a circle overlapping it for the body, and another oval for the shoulder.

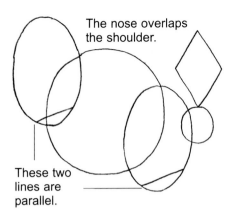

The nose overlaps the shoulder.

These two lines are parallel.

2. Draw a diamond and an oval for the head and nose. Draw two slanted lines inside the shoulder and hip ovals.

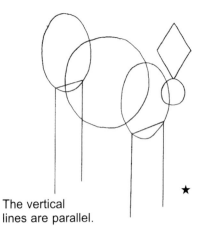

The vertical lines are parallel.

★

3. Draw four lines, one for each leg, coming from each end of the slanted lines. The lines for the legs should be parallel.

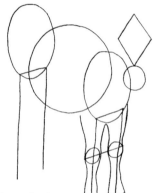

One knee looks higher than the other.

4. Draw a line parallel to the shoulder line, halfway down the front legs. Add the knees and then outline the legs.

5. Draw a line parallel to the hip line, halfway down the back legs. Add knee circles, and then outline the back legs.

★

6. Draw the rest of the outline. Add a tail. Then, erase the extra shapes and lines inside the outline.

7. Add the ears, eyes and mane. With a thin, white wax crayon, put a dot in each eye for a highlight.

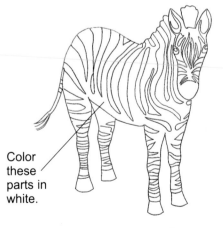

Color these parts in white.

8. Add stripes, curving them around the body. Color the white parts in wax crayon. Add white to the hooves.

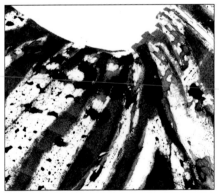

If the ink sticks to the wax stripes, scrape it off with your fingernail.

10. Paint watered-down black ink all over the zebra's body. Most of it will run off the wax, letting the white parts show.

47

Kangaroos in motion

Animals are difficult to draw in motion but can make the most exciting pictures. If you draw an animal's legs using a zigzag line (see page 12), you can just change the shape of the zigzag to draw the legs in different positions.

The zigzag changes shape as the kangaroo moves.

The lines overlapping the outline give a sense of speed.

Chalk pastels were used to draw these kangaroos.

Press very lightly.

Press harder for the back and tail.

1. Draw a big oval and a smaller oval for the body. Add a circle for the head with a wedge-shaped muzzle.

2. Draw a curve for the back and the tail. Add a big zigzag for the back leg and a smaller one for the front leg.

3. Draw an outline around the head shapes. Add the ears. Then, draw the rest of the outline, adding the legs and tail.

Lay a piece of paper over the parts you have drawn to protect them, while you do the rest of your drawing.

You will need to 'fix' this drawing so that it doesn't smudge. See page 59 for how.

To take step-by-step lessons on drawing kangaroos or some other grassland animals, visit **Art School Online**. For a link to this site, go to **www.usborne-quicklinks.com**

Your shading can go outside the outline a little.

Do all the lines in the same direction.

4. Use an orange chalk pastel to draw lots of lines all going in the same direciton. Leave some paper showing through.

5. Use a paler chalk pastel to add highlights on the kangaroo's back, tail, legs and on the head.

6. Use a darker chalk pastel to add the details to the face. Then, add shadows under the body, legs and tail.

Birds in flight

You can use the same basic shapes to draw birds in lots of different flight positions. Draw a seagull following the steps below. Then, use the flight positions section to help you draw more seagulls, and create a whole scene.

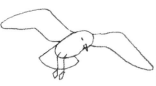

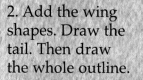

Add lines to show the bird's body.

1. In pencil, draw an oval body and a circle for a head. Draw lines to position the wings.

2. Add the wing shapes. Draw the tail. Then draw the whole outline.

3. Erase the extra lines inside the outline. Add the bird's eyes, the beak and feet.

Flight positions

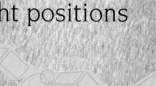

When near the ground, a bird might drop its head and let its feet hang down.

When gliding, a bird straightens its wings and tucks in its feet.

When landing, a bird tilts its wings and drops its feet.

From the front, the body looks short and the wings look narrow.

Painting the scene

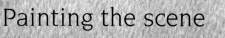

Leave the color uneven to look like clouds.

1. Dampen the paper around the birds with a brush. Then, paint a blue watercolor sky.
50

2. When the sky is dry, use pale gray watercolor to paint shadows on the birds.

3. With black watercolor, paint the eyes, and the tips of the wings and the tails.

4. Mix a little orange watercolor. Paint the beaks and feet of the birds. Let them dry.

Bird shapes

An eagle has very long, broad wings.

A swallow has angular wings and a forked tail.

A jay's body and wings are short.

You can draw different types of birds using very similar shapes to those used for drawing seagulls.

🐾 Print out bird shapes from the **Albatross Project** Web site. You can also follow steps to paint a bird's head at **John Lovett's Online Studio**, or watch a video to see how it's done. For links to these sites, go to **www.usborne-quicklinks.com**

Animals in action

As well as drawing animals in the poses shown throughout this book, you might want to draw them in other positions. You can use these drawings as reference to help you.

Eadweard Muybridge, an early photographer, took sequences of photographs like these to find out how animals move.

Dog

Sleeping

Sitting

Running

Jumping

Cat

Sleeping

Sitting

Running

Jumping

Rabbit

Grazing

Sitting up

Cleaning

Hopping

Watch animated drawings of horses in motion at **The Ultimate Horse** Web site. Also, watch a video loop made from Eadweard Muybridge's cat photographs at the **CATS! WILD TO WILD** Web site. For links to these sites, go to **www.usborne-quicklinks.com**

Horse

★

Grazing   Trotting   Rearing   Jumping

Polar bear

★

Sleeping   Walking   Rearing   Standing

Monkey

★

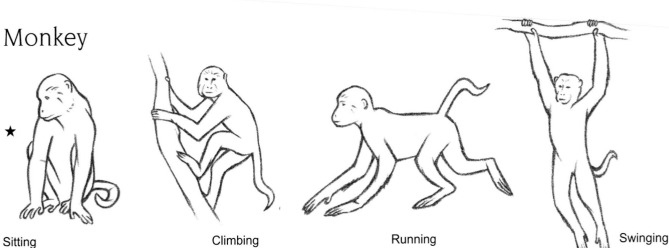

Sitting   Climbing   Running   Swinging

Animal environments

A background can add a lot to a drawing by showing where an animal is or emphasizing parts of its character. Here are some examples of the effect a choice of background can have on a picture, and tips on ways of painting backgrounds.

In this picture, the elephants' size is emphasized by their reflections in the water and by the trees behind them.

Horizon and scale

The size you draw an animal in relation to its background can make it look bigger or smaller. You can also use the horizon line (where the land and sky meet) to emphasize an animal's size.

This bear is bursting out of its background. The horizon line is very low. This makes the bear look huge.

This bear family is tiny against the hills. The horizon line is high, making the bears look like just a small part of their environment.

54

Painting a background first

1. Paint a pale watercolor wash for the background (see page 34). Leave it until it is completely dry.

2. Add an animal in a stronger color. The background color will show through, so it's best to use similar colors on top.

You could add details in colored pencil once the paint is dry.

Painting an animal first

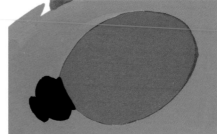

1. Paint an animal. Let it dry. Then, paint clean water onto the background, right up to the edges of the animal.

2. Paint a color wash around the animal. Don't go right up to the outline: the damp paper will carry the color up to it.

You could add an outline when it is dry, or it might look good without one.

Painting around an animal

Paint the details on top with a fine brush.

1. Draw outlines for the whole scene. Paint the background areas, overlapping the outline of the animal very slightly.

2. When the background is dry, paint the animal so that its outline overlaps the background a little.

Drawing from life

Animals are difficult to draw from life, as you can't ask them to sit still. Drawing animals you see around you is the ideal way to learn how to draw them. So, here are a few tips to help you.

David Hockney's drawing of his dogs 'Stanley and Boodgie 23 September 93' was one of many sketches and paintings he made of them.

Drawing sleepy pets

If you have a pet, then you can practice drawing it again and again. A good time to draw animals is when they are asleep because they will be keep still.

1. Draw some simple shapes and a rough outline of the animal's pose, first.

2. Add more detail to the outline once you have drawn the whole shape.

3. If the animal moves, you can still look at details, like its whiskers, and draw them.

56

Feeding time

If you visit a farm or zoo, you can draw the animals in their enclosures. Try drawing them at feeding time, when they are more likely to be all in one place and not moving around too much.

Animals that are eating tend to repeat certain movements again and again.

When drawing from life, look at the animal before you draw each line on your page. This will make your drawing more accurate.

Drawing groups

When drawing a group of animals, look at different animals in the group to catch their poses. If there's a whole group of ducks for example, you can look at lots of different birds to draw one, as they will all repeat the same poses.

Draw the animals in the front larger and with more detail than the ones in the background. Also, make the background ones paler.

Materials for drawing

What you choose to draw with and to draw on will have an effect on how your drawing looks. These pages tells you a little about materials and what effects you can get.

🐾 Find out about drawing and painting materials at the **TOYSKEMP** Web site, or take some online tutorials using various materials at the **HomeSchoolArts** Web site. For links to these sites, go to **www.usborne-quicklinks.com**

How to open Microsoft® Paint

The computer drawing program, Paint, can be found on any computer with Microsoft® Windows®. Here's how to open it.

You can draw in this white area. Find out how on pages 10-11 and 38-41.

1. Move your pointer over *Start*. Click with the left mouse button. A list will appear on your screen.

2. Move the pointer up the list to *Programs* and click. Another list will appear. Move across to *Accessories* and click.

3. On the list that appears, move the pointer to *Paint* and click. The Paint window will appear on your screen.

Paintbrushes

You can get lots of different kinds of paintbrushes which are good for different things. Soft paintbrushes (sable or synthetic) are good for using watercolors or inks. Coarser textured brushes are good with acrylic paints.

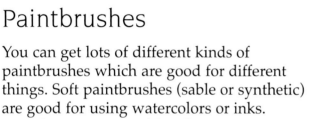

Thick brushes are good for filling in large areas of color.

Fine brushes are good for details or outlines.

Always rinse your brushes well after painting. Leaving paint on them will damage the bristles.

Pencils

Pencils come in different levels of hardness or softness. They are labelled with a number and a letter – either B (meaning soft) or H (meaning hard). The higher the number, the harder or softer the pencil. For example, 9B is very soft and 9H is very hard. HB is medium.

Soft pencils make dark, blurry lines and are good for drawing varied textures and bold images.

Hard pencils make light, thin lines and are good for drawing delicate detail.

Papers

You can use good quality cartridge paper for most things, but different types of paper are good for using with particular materials. Here are some examples.

Pastels look good on textured pastel paper. The colors look bright and blend well on the paper.

Brown wrapping paper is cheap and suitable for pastels. It gives a smooth finish.

Rough watercolor paper gives your drawings texture.

Smooth, or hotpress, watercolor paper gives a sleek finish.

Printing computer pictures onto colored paper will alter the colors.

Acrylic paints work well on thick paper or cardboard.

Fixing drawings

If you use soft pencils or chalk pastels you should 'fix' your drawing so it doesn't smudge. You can do this by spraying it with fixative spray or hairspray. Always follow the directions on the can, and fix pictures outside or somewhere with lots of fresh air.

Spray in sweeping movements going horizontally and then vertically.

Don't use too much spray.

59

Gallery

Over the next four pages you can see a gallery of animal pictures, which were drawn or painted using techniques and materials described in this book. Look through the gallery for new ideas. You can turn back to the pages mentioned to read more about certain techniques.

These three animals were drawn and painted using inks.

This penguin scene was painted in watercolors using a similar technique to the dolphin scene on pages 34-35.

This gorilla was drawn in chalk pastels, like the orangutan on page 23, but using a more realistic style.

This racoon was drawn in felt-tip pen. Then, the lines were smudged with a wet paintbrush (see page 17).

This bird's head was drawn from a photograph using pencil. The shading technique is similar to that described on page 14.

🐾 Look at different styles of animal art at the **Arts & New Media** Web site and also at the **San Diego Museum of Art** Web site. For links to these Web sites go to **www.usborne-quicklinks.com**

This toucan was drawn on a computer in Microsoft® Paint using shape tools and the brush tool (see pages 10 and 38).

This frog was painted in watercolors. The colors were blended on wet paper, in a similar way to the dolphin's bodies on page 35.

This cat was drawn and shaded in pencil, in a similar way to the dog on page 9 and the mouse on page 16.

👣 Look at an online exhibition of wildlife paintings at the **National Museum of Wildlife Art** Web site. For a link to this Web site, go to **www.usborne-quicklinks.com**

This frog was drawn on a computer using Microsoft® Paint (see pages 10 and 38).

This pig was drawn quickly using felt-tip pen. Then, the lines were smudged with a wet paintbrush (see page 17).

This chicken was painted from life using colored inks and a small brush.

These crocodiles were painted in watercolor, then outlined in felt-tip pen. The same technique was used for the hippos on pages 42-43.

This tiger was drawn in a cartoony style using watercolor and fine felt-tip pen.

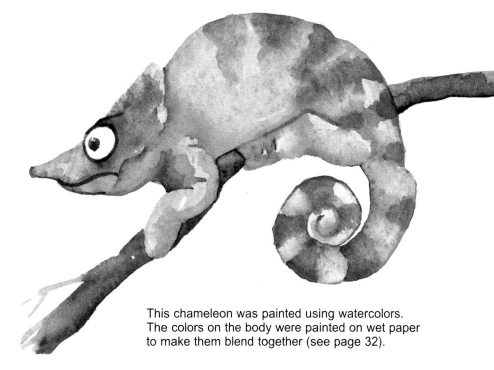

This chameleon was painted using watercolors. The colors on the body were painted on wet paper to make them blend together (see page 32).

This cow was drawn from life using white, brown and black conté crayons (which are similar to chalk pastels, see pages 20-23).

Index

★ This symbol marks pictures throughout the book which you can download to use as clip art on your computer, or print out and use to help you draw animals. To do this, go to **www.usborne-quicklinks.com** and follow the instructions.

Acknowledgements

Every effort has been made to trace the copyright holders of the material in this book. If any rights have been omitted, the publishers offer their sincere apologies and will rectify this in any subsequent editions following notification. The publishers are grateful to the following organizations and individuals for their contributions and permission to reproduce material:

Page 4 Elephant painting © Earl & Nazima Kowall/CORBIS
Page 5 Albrecht Dürer 'The Rhinoceros' 1515. Woodcut (print). © Bettmann/CORBIS; James Ward 'Adonis, King George III's Favorite Charger' c.1823-24. Lithograph © Christie's Images/CORBIS
Page 6 Red fox © Joe McDonald/CORBIS
Page 8 Leopard, rhinoceros, penguin, marmot, antelope © Digital Vision
Page 12 Pisanello, Antonio Pucci (or Pucino) 'Three cows' (detail) c. 1430-1440. Silver point, pencil and pen © PhotoRMN
Page 16 Albrecht Dürer 'A Young Hare' 1502. Watercolor and gouache on paper © SuperStock
Page 18 Ito Jakuchu 'Roosters' c.1757-67 © Sakamoto Photo Research Laboratory/CORBIS
Page 28 Henri Rousseau 'Tiger in a Tropical Storm (Surprised!)' 1891. Oil on canvas © National Gallery Collection; By kind permission of the Trustees of the National Gallery, London/CORBIS

Page 37 Edward Lear cat drawings 'Nonsense Songs and Stories', (pp. 138-141), 1894. Reference (shelfmark) Opie PP 583 © Bodleian Library, University of Oxford
Page 52 Eadweard Muybridge horse photographs. Plate 626 © Kingston Museum and Heritage Service
Page 54 Elephants © Digital Vision
Page 56 David Hockney 'Stanley and Boodgie 23 September 93' 1993. Crayon on paper. 22 1/2 x 30 1/4 © David Hockney
Page 57 Koala © Tom Brakefield/CORBIS
Screen shots on pages 10-11, 38-41, and 58 used with permission from Microsoft Corporation. Microsoft®, Microsoft® Windows® 95 and Microsoft® Paint are either registered Trade Marks or Trade Marks of Microsoft Corporation in the US and other countries. Quicktime is a Trade Mark of Apple Computer, Inc. Shockwave and Flash™ are Trade Marks of Macromedia, Inc, registered in the US and other countries. RealPlayer® is a Trade Mark of RealNetworks.

Picture researcher: Ruth King. Thanks to R. Phillips, Gillian Doherty and Brenda Gladding for providing animal photographs.